Broken But Not Forgotten

Finding Strength in Faith Through Life's Deepest Wounds

by

Gwendolyn Bain

BROKEN BUT NOT FORGOTTEN:

Finding Strength in Faith Through Life's Deepest Wounds

All rights reserved. Copyright © 2025 by LyricallyBain Publishing. No part of this publication may be reproduced, distributed, or transmitted in any form or by any means, including photocopying, recording, or other electronic or mechanical methods, or any information storage and retrieval system, without the prior written permission of the author or publisher, except in the case of brief quotations embodied in critical reviews and certain other commercial uses permitted by copyright law. For permission requests, write to the publisher at gwen@lyricallybain.com.

ISBN Paperback - 979-8-9989807-0-1

ISBN Hardcover – 979-8-9989807-1-8

LCCN – 2025910192

Edited by Naomi Books, LLC

Cover art by: Donte Lay, Robert Wilson and ThriveIn LLC

Published by LyricallyBain Publishing

Painted Post, New York

Website: https://www.lyricallybain.com

Disclaimer:

This book reflects the author's personal memories and perspective. While every effort has been made to present events accurately, some details may be subjective. The content is intended solely for informational and educational purposes. The author and publisher assume no responsibility for how readers use or interpret the material.

The resources and contact information provided were accurate as of the publication date: June 15, 2025. However, services, websites, and phone numbers may change without notice. This guide is not a substitute for professional advice, diagnosis, or treatment. The author does not endorse any listed organization or guarantee the reliability, availability, or effectiveness of the resources mentioned. Readers are encouraged to independently verify all information and exercise appropriate caution when engaging with any service.

Trigger Warning:

This book contains real life depictions of emotional content, which includes topics of abandonment, molestation, rape, physical abuse, divorce, and single parenthood. These topics may be disturbing and triggering to some readers. Please exercise caution before continuing if you feel this subject matter would be harmful to your mental or emotional well-being.

Dedication

"The truth is, everyone is going to hurt you. You just got to find the ones worth suffering for.

—Bob Marley

This book is dedicated to anyone in my life who has dropped me and caused me to be broken. It is because of you that I have grown into the strong woman I am today.

I want you to know that I forgive you. It is through these experiences and tests I've endured throughout my life that I can now use my testimony to help other young women. If any of my "business" revealed in this book can help just one person going through what I've endured, then writing this book was well worth it.

Contents

Foreword vi

Acknowledgments vii

Chapter One
    Childhood 1

Chapter Two
    The Teenage Years 8

Chapter Three
    Losing the Love of My Life 20

Chapter Four
    The Secret is Revealed 26

Chapter Five
    Longing for that Lost Love 39

Chapter Six
    The Marriage 45

Chapter Seven
    A New Start - So I Thought 54

Chapter Eight
    Life After Divorce 61

Chapter Nine
    Where the Past Ends, The Future Begins 80

Chapter Ten
    God Will Never Leave Nor Forsake You 87

Resources 95

Conclusion 97

Endorsements 101

About the Author 104

Foreword

Childhood molestation leaves deep scars that often linger into adulthood. In these pages, Gwen Bain bares her soul, sharing her journey of resilience, faith in God, and the path to healing and reclaiming one's life.

Within this book, you will encounter stories of pain and struggle, but also of hope, strength, and unwavering faith. Gwen's path to healing was not linear, and each person's journey is unique. This book aims to provide solace, understanding, and a sense of community to those who have endured similar experiences.

As you read, may you experience strength from God to confront your past, the courage to seek help, and the hope in Jesus Christ to believe in a brighter future. Remember, healing is possible, and you are not alone.

> "O Lord my God, I cried unto thee, and thou hast healed me."
> —Psalm 30:2 (King James Version)

Blessings,
Pastor Lorri A. Thornton

Acknowledgments

"Challenge Yourself - it's the only path which leads to growth."

—Morgan Freeman

I would like to thank my husband, Roger Bain, for his patience and for the love he shows me daily. He is my Boaz, and I thank God for him. Roger, I love you, and I am looking forward to spending the rest of my life with you.

To my sons, RJ, BJ, and DJ, I love you with all my heart, and I've always tried (although I haven't succeeded at times) to keep you from being "dropped." You are my life, and I thank God every day for allowing me to be your mother. I know I always tell you this, but I want you and the world to know and always remember—as long as I have breath in my body, I will be here for you. I love you all!

To Wendy Ward, I thank you for showing me what true friendship looks like. Meeting you back in 1996 and getting to know you was a godsend. You've been there throughout my adulthood highs and the lowest of my lows. Through it all, you never judged me or my situation. You've always been a prayer warrior and someone I knew would shoot straight from the hip with any advice you gave me. Although sometimes the advice was hard to swallow, you always had me look at it from God's perspective. I am truly thankful for you and the friendship/sistership we share.

To the Bouies and Councils, what can I say? You were there for me and my boys in my darkest hours. You all loved on us like we were blood relatives, and the bond we shared exemplified what family and true friendship were all about. There were some days when I didn't know if I was coming or going, but you always demonstrated to me through love and actions that you had my back. I am forever indebted to you. I thank God for using you to illustrate to me what unconditional love was all about.

To Janice Rawlings (my coach), I offer up a sincere, from the heart, "Thank You!" You were one of the few adults in my childhood who didn't drop me. Lord knows I was more than a handful during my teenage years, but you never let that stop you from showing me you cared. All those countless hours you spent talking to a hardheaded teenager with a bad attitude, just listening to me vent, meant the world to me. You were definitely a godsend in a season when I needed it most.

I want to thank my childhood friend Joann Chester (Jones). *Giiiiirrrrrrl,* we had some *times*! Some good and some bad, but through it all, we remained steadfast, and we are friends to this day. I remember the first time you told me I needed to write a book and my "Yeah, right" response. You obviously knew something I didn't know at the time. It wasn't long after that when God put this book in my spirit. I thank you for being obedient and sensitive to who and what God has called you to be.

Endless gratitude to Donte Lay and Robert Wilson for turning my book cover vision into reality. Your artistry and dedication mean the world—thank you!

Last, but certainly not least, I want to thank my village. Anyone who helped me as I struggled through my darkest hours and helped me with my boys… I thank you. I thank those to whom I sent the draft of this book to read, reread, and read again. Your input was valuable and appreciated.

Lord, use me now to motivate, encourage, and inspire young women to love You. By loving You, they will come to love themselves.

Chapter One

Childhood

"A winner is a dreamer who never gives up."
—Nelson Mandela

I was born on December 17th in Westbury, New York. That's on Long Island, for those of you who are not familiar with the area. I was the second oldest of four children living in a single-parent household. I had two brothers and one sister, and we all had different fathers.

I was the oldest girl. As a little girl growing up in poverty in the suburbs of New York, dreaming was all one could do at times. You see, I dreamed of escaping the hurt that filled my childhood. I was broken for so many reasons, and you will soon discover why. I dreamed of being married, having a *real* family that consisted of a husband, kids, a house with a white picket fence, and the ability to afford board games and food for my family.

The dream that seemed to overwhelm or consume my thought process was that of my dad. I often wondered where my dad was and why he would allow me to be subjected to this kind of life. An even better question was, "Who is my dad?" What type of person would father a child and have absolutely nothing to do with them? *What was wrong with me that a man could father me and then not want anything to do with me?*

I looked at my friends whose fathers were in their lives, and I wanted that so much. I can remember telling myself that I would never do this to my kids. *When I get married, it will be "until death do us part." I will never get a divorce.*

Life at the Jones household left a lot to be desired—well, for me at least. I grew up watching my mother parade different men in and out of the house at will. I remember times when she thought my brothers and I were asleep, and in came her next… well, I won't say it. The door to her room would close, and it would get quiet. *Squeak, squeak! Squeak, squeak!* The sound of the bed begging for mercy. The moans and groans that filled the night air left little doubt as to what was going on behind that door.

I recall a particular night when I was in the fourth grade. My sister's father came over, and the door to the room closed. About an hour or so later, he left. To my surprise, minutes later, in walks my brother's father. And guess what? The door closed, and the bed started "crying" again. That bed got a true workout that night. Oh, it was pretty much most nights, but two different men in the same night, within minutes of each other, was something new.

As if her children seeing all the different men in and out of her bedroom was not enough, my mom never seemed to have time for her kids, or at least that's how *I* felt. She was consumed with herself and the things she wanted to do. Don't get me wrong, my mom worked, but she was always in the street running from this card game to that card game, going to the racetrack, playing numbers, partying, and drinking. She would leave us with anyone who would say they would babysit for her, including a sixteen-year-old boy whose hormones were raging.

We knew that no matter who she left us with, we had better behave because she did *not* play when it came to discipline. If someone told her we misbehaved, we would get the beating of a lifetime. Heck, half the time we were in public with her, all she had to do was look at us, and we knew whatever we were doing had better be corrected immediately. One would have to wonder if in the backwoods of Sardis,

Mississippi (where my mom was born), they held a camp to teach Mississippians how to whoop their kids. *Just kidding!*

I was a nightmare in school. I stayed in trouble. I would fight at the drop of a dime, and it didn't matter who it was I was fighting. If you spoke to me and I thought you were trying to disrespect me, I would have no problem fighting you. I remember one day I was getting off the bus at school. I was in the fifth grade, and a girl made a comment to me. I literally pushed her through the plate glass door that was at the entrance of the school. Of course, I got suspended, but who cared? No one cared about me, so I cared about no one.

I had a *fresh* mouth, and I couldn't care less about school. I was hurting and broken, and I lashed out at anything and anybody. I didn't care. Throughout elementary school, I did just enough work in school to have a "C" average, and this often infuriated my teachers. I can recall attending parent-teacher conferences, and the teachers would tell my mom I was capable of so much more, but I wouldn't apply myself.

Making friends did not come easily for me because trusting people and believing they sincerely cared for me did not exist in my world. I would later see this as ironic, because I was always trying to find a man who would love me, and I believed he would care. I ruined a lot of friendships because of a lack of trust and a poor attitude. Even as a child, I would tell people quickly, "I can be your best friend or your worst enemy, so don't cross me."

For years, I blamed my mom for the warped outlook I had on life. A parent is supposed to protect their children at all costs, no matter what. *How do you continuously subject your children to poisonous environments?* I don't get it. I was angry at the world for what I had gone through, and I never learned how to cope with it properly.

Chapter One – Childhood
Thoughtful Reflection

1. Have you ever felt abandoned by the people you felt should have been there for you? _____

    If yes, how have you dealt with your feelings toward this person or these people? _____

    _____
    _____
    _____
    _____
    _____
    _____
    _____
    _____
    _____
    _____
    _____
    _____
    _____

Childhood

2. As a child, were you put in dangerous or "poisonous" environments you didn't know how to handle? _____

If yes, what type of situations were they? Looking back, can you pinpoint the warnings and red flags an adult should have protected you from?

_____
_____
_____
_____

If yes, how did you cope with being in these negative or harmful environments? _____

_____
_____

Was the effect of being in these environments reflected in your behavior then? _____. If so, how? _____

_____
_____

Is it reflected in your behavior now? _____

If so, how? _____

_____
_____

Chapter Two

The Teenage Years

"You don't always need to understand your journey in life,
you just need to trust that you're going in the right direction."

—Steven Aitchison

As a preteen and teenager, I buried myself in any activity at school that allowed me to stay away from home. I went to school at 7:30 a.m. and would often not return home until 11:00 p.m. I was in the drama club, chorus, and honor society, and I played any sport there was to be played. Yeah, you heard right, I said "Honor Society."

When I was in eighth grade, my mother sent me to South Carolina to stay with my brother's grandmother. That was the summer from hell. My brother's grandmother was a tyrant, and we were her slaves. All day, we had to cook, clean, and watch her spit tobacco snuff across the room into her tin can. How disgusting! Every time my mother called to check on us, she would tell my mother that I kept an attitude because she would not "let this guy get into my bird cage" (read between the lines). I was livid with her because I was not interested in having sex with this guy, and believe me, if I wanted to do it, there were plenty of opportunities to do so.

My mom threatened to leave me in South Carolina because of my behavior and bad attitude. I told her that if she allowed me to come home, I would be an honor student. And yes, I was on the honor roll from ninth grade through twelfth grade. There was no way on God's green earth I could have stayed in South Carolina with that woman. One of us would have ended up in jail or dead, and I am not kidding.

When it came to sports, I had natural talent. I found sports to be a way of escape for me. I played sports at schools and at our local park. When teams were formed for softball at my local park, I made it my business to be there for sign-ups. I played softball in the women's adult league at the age of twelve. Sports consumed me. You see, as long as my mind was on sports, I didn't have to think about my childhood and my messed-up life. As I played sports and excelled at them, people never knew the hurt that dwelled within me. I *did* have a very bad attitude, but few took the time to try to find out what was actually going on with me. They saw an individual with a drive to be the best in sports, but she had a poor attitude.

Truth be told, I wouldn't have shared with them what was going on with me anyway, because I had been warned not to say anything. Well, let me correct that; I *did* have one gym teacher (coach) whom I confided in. I basically told her what I wanted her to know and made it my business not to reveal the one secret that was consuming my life. I told her how unhappy I was at home, how my mother and I really didn't get along, and how I sometimes wish I had not been born or wished I were dead. To this day, I am so grateful that God placed her in my life because I know there were several times she talked me down from doing something crazy.

I was promiscuous and drank heavily as another way to escape the torment consuming my life. It wasn't like I wanted to have intercourse or even enjoyed it; I was looking more for acceptance than the feel of the moment. I wanted someone to love me for *me*. Yes, and with each guy I had, I thought it was love. Man, did I need a reality check. They got what they wanted and often moved on when they felt they needed something different. Don't get me wrong, I had some relationships that lasted for months or a year, and others that went as quickly as they came. My motto was never to fight over a man. I had many opportunities to do so, though. When I was in junior high school, girls would come up to me and ask if I was dating so and so, and I would tell them, "Yeah, but if you want him, you can have him. There are plenty of fish in the sea." I guess you can say I didn't have a sense of loyalty. I don't know if it was that or if I had zero tolerance for men cheating on me. I would rather let them go than be hurt by them. Now, I see that I was just protecting myself.

Drinking was my crutch, and I did it every chance I got. I can remember being in seventh grade, going to first-period math (8:00 in the morning), with Pepsi and Bacardi or Johnnie Walker Red in a bottle—sitting in the front row, drinking in class. This would be grounds for immediate expulsion in schools today. Well, I probably would not have gotten into too much trouble at home since my mom's favorite motto was "I would rather you drink at home than be out in the street drinking; at least I know what you're doing."

Drinking was my way of coping. I loved playing sports throughout my school years, but you had better believe that after every sporting event, I had a drink waiting for me. Typically, my sports teams would gather at my house after a game because they knew my mom would allow us to drink and have fun without telling their parents. To say we abused alcohol would be an understatement. Once, six of us got together at the junior high football field and drank eighteen quarts of different beers. Some of my friends were so drunk that we literally had to carry them home and put them in bed.

Having sex while I was on a buzz from the alcohol was addictive. I loved the sense of someone having their way with me and me pleasing them. *Oh, this is definitely love*, I thought. *I see why my mom has all of these different men coming in and out of the house.* As I look back at these times, I thank God I did not become an alcoholic. With all the drinking and giving my body to the different men who showed me attention, I am thankful to God that I am not dead or living with AIDS.

In high school, I had two serious relationships. The first was with TB. (I'll use initials to keep from revealing the individuals, but you know who you are.) I met him at a party in Roslyn that our girls' basketball team attended. We danced the night away, and then he asked me if he could drive me home. Because he was a friend of one of my teammates, I said, "Okay." The next morning, my teammate called me and said he liked me and wanted to know if he could get my number. Of course, I said, "Yes."

This became my first *real* relationship. I truly cared for him and thought I was going to spend the rest of my life with him. We did everything together. We went to the movies, to basketball games, hung out at the park, and simply enjoyed being together. We found places to be intimate. It didn't matter where it was; if the urge was there, it happened. *I have finally found what I've dreamed of for so many years—someone who was willing to love me for me*—or at least, that's what I thought.

I remember the day when my world was turned upside down. I was walking down Railroad Avenue, and he drove up and told me he needed to talk to me. He said, "Gwen, do you remember the other night when I called you _____?" (Yes, you guessed it, someone else's name.) He continued, "Well, she was my ex-girlfriend. I went to see her the other night."

I must have blanked out for the next few minutes because I don't remember any of the in-between conversation. The next thing I remember saying was, "It's over," and that was it. An entire year of my life had been wasted on him. He tried to get back in, but the trust factor was gone. We "kicked it" when we needed intimacy, but it was never the same.

My next love, or should I say "standing" relationship, was with DL (Long Island's number one player). I thought the world revolved around him and felt I could not live without him. My every thought was of him. I slept, ate, and practically lived at his house during twelfth grade. I was so hooked on him that I began to ignore my childhood friends, family, and teammates. The only person I wanted to be around was him. He would say, "Jump," and I would say, "How high, how high?" We never did much together other than watch movies, drink, watch TV, party, and be intimate. Wow, I actually thought I was in love! I just knew I was going to spend the rest of my life with him. I was wrong again.

The day came when he returned from visiting his family in Alabama, and he blew up because I was at my house with my brother and cousin, drinking. He broke up with me! I drank all the time, and he knew this. *Why was he so upset? How could he just leave me?* I was distraught, and literally felt my world had come to an end.

I remember crying through my entire geometry final exam the next day. My principal pulled me out of the test and sent for my coach. They tried to reassure me that everything was going to be alright, but at the moment, I needed to get through that test. I dried my eyes, went back to the test, and started crying all over again. Needless to say, I failed the final. Thank God I was carrying an "A" average beforehand, so I still ended up passing the class.

I imagine you might want to know what DL's "real deal" was, and so did I. Later, I came to find out. He did not tell me, but I heard it on the streets. What a coward! While he was in Alabama, he had hooked up with his old girlfriend. He had used my "drinking too much" as an excuse for his anger and for breaking up with me! He ended up marrying her about a month or two later. I hated him for that, and I even thought about sending him rocks as a wedding present, but I didn't.

Throughout this ordeal, I had become friends with another individual, and he truly helped me through a lot of the pain I felt from my breakup with DL. He, too, was going through a hard time in his relationship, and we became sounding boards for each other. While he was "as fine as wine," I never saw him as a boyfriend or a lover. To me, he was a friend. We sat on my mom's porch daily, talking for hours on end about everything and anything. We laughed, cried, and enjoyed one another's company. It seemed as if he truly understood me, and I understood him. He knew when I was down or upset, and he knew what to do to change that mood. For months, this man never tried to kiss me or bed me. He respected me, and I respected the fact that he was still in a relationship.

How well I remember the day his relationship came to a final head. He had just stopped by, and we were sitting on the steps of my mom's porch, and his girl walked up, threatening me. Please note, I have not been saved all my life, and I was a true fighter. I looked at him and told him, "You better get your girl because if I get up, I am going to kick her a** ." (Well, you know what came out.) He got up and tried to deal with the situation. He took her to his house, and she decided she wanted to fight him. He ended up putting her out of his house and breaking things off with her. I later went to see if he was okay. As usual, we ended up back at my mom's house, sitting on the porch and discussing the happenings of the day. We remained the best of friends, and we grew closer.

I cannot say at what point we actually became an item, but I can truly say he was my best friend. He was my world. I believed I had finally found someone who knew me and loved me for *me*. It was different this time. I knew I would spend the rest of my life with this man, and we discussed this often. I had searched for love for years, and he was the love of my life. I loved him more than words could ever express—heck, more than life itself. We were so good together in that we truly *knew* each other. We clicked so well that we could complete each other's thoughts and words before they were even spoken.

We never got tired of being around each other. I remember us going to the park, playing basketball and softball together, watching TV, sitting on my mom's porch just talking, walking and holding hands, drinking, and even more memorable than all that was when we made love. I had never cried before when a man made love to me. My tears were not because of pain or him physically hurting me. Actually, he was unbelievably gentle with me. Being with him was like an out-of-body experience because we would both be moved to tears as we expressed our love for each other. There was a connection between us that I had never felt, and I have not felt with anyone else since. I remember telling him that I never wanted to lose him. I truly believed he was my soulmate, and he is definitely the only man I have ever been *IN LOVE* with.

Chapter Two – The Teenage Years
Thoughtful Reflection

1. Have you ever found yourself being promiscuous, seeking the acceptance or love of a man? _____

    If so, do you feel this behavior may have been because of not having a father figure in your life? _____

    How do you feel about this today? _____

    _____
    _____
    _____
    _____
    _____

    How could this also apply to other situations you've experienced? _____

    _____
    _____
    _____
    _____

The Teenage Years

2. Have you ever turned to alcohol, drugs, sex, etc., to help you through challenging situations you encountered in life? _____

If so, how could these things have actually hurt you instead? _____

_____

_____

_____

_____

_____

_____

_____

_____

_____

_____

_____

_____

Chapter Three

Losing the Love of My Life

"Slow down and enjoy the journey right now.
Take time for the people in your life.
They won't always be there."

—Joel Osteen

I was now eighteen, going on nineteen, and about to go off to college. My school was six hours away from my hometown. I had never been away from home for any extended period without my brothers, so I did not know what to expect. We had typically gone south together to Mississippi for the summer as young kids. This was different. I had finally found a man who truly loved me, and I was about to leave him. *Our love is strong enough to endure this. We will make it,* I told myself.

It was my freshman year. I spent hours nightly on the phone conversing with him. I just wanted to be in his arms and have him hold me like I had grown accustomed to. I missed him so much!. We cried together and constantly expressed how much we missed each other. The pain of being away from this man was unreal. I remember running up my phone bill and him sending me money to pay it, along with stamps, so I would not have an excuse for not writing to him. He would also send me spending money because he knew my mom was not in a position to provide that for me. On Valentine's Day in 1985, he purchased a big box of Valentine candy that weighed at least 30 pounds, and with it came a friendship/promise ring. I was happier than a frog on a log.

Because everything sounds so perfect, one might ask at this point, "Well, what happened?" I'll tell you. Summer 1985 came, and I was home from college. My mom and his cousin kept telling me how I needed to find someone who was on my level—someone who desired to do the things I wanted to do—someone with goals. "All he wants to do is play basketball," said my mom. She ignored the fact that he had a full-time job, and he was taking care of me and my bills while I was at school. I listened to this for a good portion of the summer. It began to wear me down. I knew I loved him, but all the negative talk made me doubt him and question myself. *Did I need to be with someone who had more stability?*

And then the day came when an Army man asked me out after one of my softball games. I was flattered, so I accepted. *But how could I go on a date with someone else when the man I loved lived next door?*

Because I had never cheated on anyone I ever dated, I didn't want to start then. Being young and dumb, I decided to break up with my boyfriend instead. I remember that night as if it were yesterday.

When I told him it was over, he cried. He held me down on his bed and pleaded with me not to break up with him.

"Pooh, please don't do this, please don't. I love you. Whatever I've done wrong, I will fix it. Please don't break up with me!"

I gave him his ring back and left. My decision was final. He tried to talk to me, but I wouldn't give him the time of day, even though I really wanted to. Weeks passed by, and though I longed to be with him, my pride would not let me go back. I've since learned that being prideful can cause you to lose out on blessings God has for you. The hurt of losing my best friend and soulmate has had a residual effect on my ability to love completely.

I ended up cheating on the Army guy, and I didn't care. He was thirty-five, and I was nineteen. Boy, was that a mistake. All he wanted to do was bed me, play softball, and tell me what girls' softball team he wanted me to play on. He never wanted to go anywhere or do anything other than have sex. I was nineteen years old, stuck in the world of a thirty-five-year-old I knew nothing about.

Neither life nor relationships got any better for me. I began to drink even more and party with people who were more my age. The saga of different men and my search to find someone to love me continued. The guy I cheated with was married, but I cared about this man. I often wondered when he actually slept with his wife because we were always in some hotel getting busy. The strange part of it all was that I knew his wife, and we were often at softball games and cookouts together.

When I went back to Rochester to go to college, we stayed on the phone talking, and when I came home for school breaks, you could bank on the fact that we were going to hook up as soon as I was in town. It's interesting to me now how we kept our relationship hidden from the rest of our teammates (he played on the men's softball team, and I played on the women's team).

The more I was with him, the more I desired to be with him. Finally, I knew I had to end the relationship when I started having dreams of being caught. His best friend kept telling me that I was "messing with his head," and I had him all confused. The last thing I wanted to do was to destroy his home. I didn't want to be the cause of him leaving his wife, or did I? *Hmmm*, I was young; I cannot really say I wouldn't have welcomed him back with open arms.

Well, the summer of 1985 was over, and I was back at college. Guys, guys, guys… so many to choose from! I hated dating guys my age. My thought process was: *Why is this individual always jockeying me? Okay, I'll hang out with him… for now. We can be friends until a better prospect comes around.*

Chapter Three – Losing the Love of My Life
Thoughtful Reflection

1. Have you ever given up a person who treated you like a queen because you felt you weren't worthy of their love? If so, what was the impact of that experience? _____

   _____

   _____

   _____

   _____

   _____

   What were your feelings at the time? _____

   _____

   _____

   _____

   _____

   What did you do to help you cope with the loss? _____

   _____

   _____

   _____

Chapter Four

The Secret is Revealed

"I am not what happened to me. I am what I choose to become."

—Carl Jung

It was two weeks before Thanksgiving break, and a classmate and I were sitting in the student lounge at my college watching a movie. Tears were beginning to flow, and I told myself, "I've got to stop them. Surely no one sees my tears," or at least I thought not.

Out of the blue, I heard my classmate ask, "Gwen, what's wrong with you?"

I replied, "Nothing."

"Yes, there is something. You wouldn't be sitting here crying if nothing was wrong."

I contemplated... *do I tell him?* He was a friend, but I had harbored this secret for thirteen years. Besides, I didn't

The Secret is Revealed

want to get into trouble with my mom. *No, no, I can't tell him! What's happening? What… what am I saying?*

"I… I… I was molested."

You see, the movie we were watching was dealing with kids who were being molested, and it brought up so many of the ill feelings I had suppressed for years. As my friend looked at me in a state of disbelief, I poured out my soul.

I told him how my mother would constantly have this 16-year-old boy (SM) babysit us when she wanted to go out. He was having his way with me. The abuse started at the age of five and continued until I was nine. We often spent the night at his grandmother's house, and sometimes two or three times a night, he would wake me up and force me to get into his bed so he could have sex with me. I'm talking full penetration and ejaculation! As I shared with him, it dawned on me that I was calling it "having sex." I was just a child. No, it wasn't "sex!" He raped me! He molested me!

There were nights when I would fall asleep in his grandmother's room, and I felt, "Thank God! I am safe tonight." Then, it never failed—he would come into her room, wake me up, and make me follow him to his room. Other times, he would make a palette for me and my brothers on his bedroom floor. When he saw that they were asleep, he would make me get into his bed. I wonder if they ever saw or knew he was doing this to me. If they did, they never said anything. Maybe they didn't even care. When I reflect upon this time of my life, I'm grateful that my sister hadn't been born yet. I would hate to think of him abusing her as well.

I can recall times when he would ejaculate inside of me, which gave me a sensation I couldn't explain at that age. Later, I realized it was my body's physical response to what was being done to me. There were other times when he would pull out, lay his penis on my stomach, and ejaculate all over me. He seemed to get a kick out of this. He would then make me get up, go into the bathroom, and wash his sperm off my body.

When I returned, he would always threaten, "You better not tell anybody because if you do, I'm gonna tell your mother what *you* did." I was terrified of getting whooped by my mother. I was young and ignorant, and I didn't realize I hadn't done anything wrong. He used my fear of my mother to paralyze me into remaining a victim for four years.

Women, it is the fear that cripples so many of us and we go through life broken and unable to cope.

If I had been menstruating during these four years, I would have gotten pregnant. He penetrated me and climaxed inside of me like I was a grown woman. It hurt so much, and I hated myself! I hated myself for letting it happen. I hated myself because I could do nothing to make it stop. I hated my mother for putting me in that environment.

I used to cry and carry on so badly when my mom would say that SM was babysitting us. She never asked me why I was crying or why I didn't want to go to SM's house, and that was because she didn't care. All she cared about was that she had a babysitter for the night, and she was going to be able to do what she wanted to do. Finally, at the age of nine, I had carried on so much that she asked her friend, AJ, and my brother's grandmother to babysit me.

I also told him about a particular night when I was at my brother's grandmother's house asleep, and I woke up to her boyfriend's hand down my pants and him trying to get his penis out. He was drunk, and that was probably the only thing that kept him from penetrating me. I pushed his hand off of me and ran downstairs to the basement where my brothers were sleeping.

I was a child, and the very people who should have been protecting me were violating me. *Where was my mother? Better yet, where was my father? Heck, who is my father?* Again, I ask, "How can a man father a child and refuse to have anything to do with her"? All these thoughts were now going through my head as I shared what had happened to me.

Afterward, my friend held me and said, "Gwen, you've got to tell your mother. This is horrible. You didn't do anything wrong, and you can't keep blaming yourself."

While the thought of telling her terrified me, I knew he was right—she needed to know. The question was, "How would I tell her?"

It was the day after Thanksgiving, and I was back home on Long Island in my mom's room, sitting on her bed.

"Mom, can I talk to you for a minute?" My heart was racing, and I could feel the wavering of my voice. "I, I... um, I need to tell you something."

"What is it?" she asked.

"Um... um... (as the tears begin to flow).

"Um, um, what?" she asked.

I was now fully engulfed in tears. "I, I, I... was molested."

"By who? When?" she yelled.

I said, "By SM. It started when I was five and continued until I was nine. I used to cry and beg you not to send me over there, but you didn't care! You just kept sending me over there for him to do this to me," I said. "I told you I didn't want to go over there!"

She began to cry, saying she didn't know. I told her that she wasn't *trying* to know. "All you wanted to do was party, play cards, and go to the racetrack. I begged you to let somebody else keep me, but you didn't allow that until I was nine."

She then said, "I often wondered why you were crying, but I had no idea it was *that*."

I remember thinking, *if you wondered why I was crying, you should have asked me what was going on, as opposed to sending me over there anyway.*

As she began to weep uncontrollably, she told me that she, too, had been molested. She informed me that my grandfather (her father) molested her every chance he got, and that is why she left home at the age of eighteen. She told me she was sorry, and she never meant for this to happen to me.

I felt as if a weight had been lifted from me, but then I was left not knowing how to move on from that point. I was still lost. I was a young woman who needed love. I had never experienced the love from my father that should have set the standard for what *real* love should be. I longed for that special love from a man. I didn't know how to process all I felt on my own.

One thing was clear to me: SM was a predator. *That* wasn't love. My mom didn't offer to take me to counseling, so life went on as usual, with me suppressing what I was feeling inside and suffering from it alone.

During the summer of my junior year in college, my cousin and I went to the predator's grandmother's house. (My cousin was picking up his son.) The predator cornered me in the bathroom and said, "Hey, if you ever want to hook up, just let me know."

I looked at him and said, "M****r F****r, I am *not* that child you molested. I will kill you if you ever touch me again."

A righteous indignation rose up in me, and I was dead serious. I would have given up my freedom to bury this individual. I do not promote violence, nor am I telling anyone to take this course of action, but at that moment, I had to stand up for myself.

Chapter Four – The Secret is Revealed
Thoughtful Reflection

1. Were you sexually abused (molested or raped) as a child, teenager, or adult? _____

   If so, did you tell anyone? _____

   Did you feel like you had a voice and someone would listen? _____

   _____

   _____

   _____

   _____

   _____

   _____

   _____

   _____

   _____

   _____

   _____

   _____

2. Is it possible you're still suffering from this trauma? ____

   If so, what are you experiencing? _____

   _____

   _____

   _____

   _____

   _____

   If so, have you ever sought professional help to deal with it? _____

   If yes, what was the result? _____

   _____

   _____

   _____

   _____

   _____

   _____

   _____

   _____

3. Have you seen (had to face) the perpetrator? _____

    If so, what did you do? _____

    _____

    _____

    _____

    _____

    _____

    _____

    _____

    How did it make you feel? _____

    _____

    _____

    _____

    _____

    _____

    _____

    _____

    _____

    _____

4. In what ways has this trauma impacted your life? _____

_____
_____
_____
_____
_____
_____
_____
_____
_____
_____
_____
_____
_____
_____
_____
_____
_____
_____
_____
_____
_____
_____

5. Do you find it difficult to trust or love someone with your "whole heart?"

___

6. As a child or teenager, did you tell an adult that you had been molested or raped? _____. If so, were you believed? _____

   Did you receive support? _____

   If so, what actions were taken? _____
   _____
   _____
   _____

   If you were not believed, what was said and done? _____
   _____
   _____
   _____

   How did you respond to what transpired? _____
   _____
   _____
   _____

   How did this make you feel? _____
   _____
   _____
   _____
   _____

Chapter Five

Longing for that Lost Love

"When you lose someone you love, they never really leave you.
They just move into a special place in your heart."
—Catherine O'Hara

I had revealed the secret that had plagued me for thirteen years, and I was still unhappy and alone. I was then a senior in college and about to graduate. I was beginning to feel as if there was more to life than partying, drinking, and being promiscuous. All the while, I was thinking of the man I truly loved. *Why did I give him up?* My life would be so different now if we had stayed together. I had listened to my mother and his cousin who took pride in parading men in and out of their houses and bedrooms. Love could have slapped them in the face, and they wouldn't have known it. Opening their legs to any and everybody was their greatest satisfaction. They had no idea how I felt about him, and yet I allowed them to influence me to break up with him. Man, how I missed him!

After I graduated from college, I moved back to my mom's house so I could find a job and get myself established. I was still thinking about him. I asked his cousin several times if she could get me a number or an address so I could call or write him. I wanted to let him know how sorry I was for the way I ended our relationship. She never gave me this information. I can only gather she was jealous of what we had, or she truly didn't want me with him. I guess I will never know her reason.

I had a few more relationships after graduation, and the dating scene was beginning to get old. I learned that sex isn't love, and love is just a word when you are with the wrong person. I wanted, I needed, and I believed I would one day have a man in my life to love me and complete me.

No, no Lord, this cannot be happening to me!

I was twenty-five and had just found out I was pregnant. Ironically, I played an April Fool's prank on my mom, brothers, and cousins—I told them I was pregnant. I was joking with them, but the joke was on me because I really *was* pregnant.

Longing for that Lost Love

My mom's opinion of my baby's father was that he was a gigolo, and she asked me what I wanted with him. Lord, if I had only listened! Hindsight is definitely 20/20!

Chapter Five – Longing for that Lost Love
Thoughtful Reflection

1. Has pride or the trauma you experienced in your life kept you from apologizing for behaviors you knew were wrong?

2. Have you ever allowed the perception or opinions of others to dictate your actions, even though you knew what they were saying was *not* what was best for you? _____
If so, what was the situation? _____

_____

_____

_____

_____

_____

_____

_____

_____

_____

_____

_____

_____

_____

_____

_____

_____

3. Is there anything you would do differently today if someone offers you advice that may go against how you feel or what you think is best for you?

_____
_____
_____
_____
_____
_____
_____
_____
_____
_____
_____
_____
_____
_____
_____
_____

Chapter Six

The Marriage

"As much as others may need to change, or we may want them to change, the only person we can continually inspire, prod, and shape –
with any degree of success – is the person in the mirror."

—Kerry Patterson

It was finally happening. My dreams were coming true. I was twenty-six, raising my first child, and marrying the father. I remember my pastor's wife asking me, on my wedding day, if I was sure I wanted to do this. All I could think was, I am not going to be like my mother. The truth was, I was not in love with the man I was about to marry. I had love for him, but I only married him because I had his child. The fantasy of marrying somebody who was going to love me—the man I was going to be with for the rest of my life—

consumed my every thought. I was in heavenly bliss. Everything was simply beautiful. The flower girl, the bridal party, the groomsmen, and my future husband were fierce, and, of course, so was I. The day was exhausting and very long. Some things went quite well, and others left much to be desired, but we made it through. Already having had a child out of wedlock didn't leave much to the imagination on the wedding night. Who cared? I had him.

We were on our way to Aruba for the honeymoon! Somehow, we actually ended up in Orlando. He had lied. How had he deceived me for months by telling me we were going to Aruba, only to find out after I married him that we were going to Orlando? I was upset! I managed to get over it, and we enjoyed the honeymoon.

Our life back in our first apartment was about to begin. I loved this man because he took care of his family. He was indeed a class "A" workaholic, or at least I thought this was the case. About six or seven months into our marriage, the real hubby began to reveal himself. First, it was 10:00 p.m. Then 11:00 p.m.... 2:00 a.m.... 5:00 a.m. *This nigga has not come home. Oh, I am not going to stand for this! It is over.* I packed his bags and called his mother and told her to tell him he could come pick them up. I was not going to allow him to disrespect me in this manner. Of course, he came with a half-baked excuse, which I didn't believe, and I ended up having to call the police to get him out of the apartment. But stupid me—I ended up taking him back because I had his child, and I wanted my family.

The arguments about his whereabouts began to occur more frequently. I remember having one big blowout. I went to work and then to church. When I arrived home that evening, I remember praying as I sat in the car. "No weapon formed against me shall prosper. Lord, You are my protection. I thank You that Your angels are encamped around and about me to protect me from all hurt, harm, and danger. Greater is He that is in me than he that is in the world."

Well, what happened next should have been enough to make anybody with common sense leave. I walked into the apartment, and it was pitch dark. None of the light switches in the front of the apartment were working. When I got to the hallway, I flipped on the light switch, and there was my husband sitting in the hallway with his Air Force switchblade knife. I stepped past him and put my son in his bed. My husband then came into the room, pushed me up against the closet door, and grabbed me around my throat. With the knife in his hand, he said, " I will kill you." I continued to pray loudly, and he eventually let me go and left the room. I couldn't do anything but cry and thank God for His divine protection.

Two and a half years passed by, and I continued to endure the mental and emotional abuse. He still came and went as he pleased. Worse yet, we moved into a different house, and I didn't know anyone around me. As if that wasn't enough to handle, I was six months pregnant with my second child. I knew he was seeing someone else; I wasn't crazy. I found cigarettes and cigarette butts with lipstick around my house. When I came in from work, my bed was messed up. To top it off, I saw a female driving his car.

I confronted him, and he became irate. He calmed down, and then he wanted to make love to me. When I refused, I experienced my second round of domestic violence; this time it was more severe. He choked me and flipped me over the bed onto the floor. I was six months pregnant. He started punching me in the face repeatedly, and I ran out of the house half-naked to the neighbors' apartment downstairs. She allowed me to call the police. When we returned to the apartment, he had gone, but not before calling his mother, who sent his brother over to the house. I discovered that my eldest son, who was three at the time, witnessed all of this. I packed my bags and off to my mother's house I went. She was very upset. I went to the hospital and remained there until 6:00 a.m. I left the hospital, went to my mom's house, changed my clothes, and then went to work. That was one of the hardest days of my life. I tried hard to cover the black eye and the bruises, but it wasn't that easy. I ended up going home sick. I left my husband and moved in with my mother. At this point in my life, I was done with this marriage.

Almost two months passed, and I got the worst news anybody could get. I was at work, and I received a call telling me that I needed to get to the hospital. My oldest brother had been admitted, and it was not looking good. I left work, and when I got to the hospital, I waited in the waiting room for what seemed like hours for the doctors. Then came the news we were not ready for. "I'm sorry we've done all we could; we've lost him." My brother had passed away.

I was eight months pregnant. I lost it emotionally. I cried uncontrollably. It's hard to believe, but the darned doctor tried to have me admitted to the mental ward. I was grieving! Heck, he was the one who was crazy. *Dude, I just lost my brother, and you're telling me I can't cry?* My mother and younger brother calmed me down by telling me that I was hurting the baby.

I was grieving. I wonder how many people know that grieving has a way of making you vulnerable. I learned that the hard way. Yes, I know—stupid me. I allowed my abuser of a husband back into my life. He was there for me during my brother's homegoing service, and he made sure I had everything I needed. He then informed me that he had been offered a job in Georgia, and he said he wanted his family. He wanted me and the kids to come with him to Georgia. I agreed. Because of my own history of neglect, I could not let go of the desire for my children to be with their father.

Since I was eight months pregnant, we decided that I would stay in New York and have the baby. Then, I would come to Georgia when the doctors told me that I could travel. He was going to go ahead and move our belongings to Georgia and find a place for us to live.

Chapter Six – The Marriage
Thoughtful Reflection

1. Have you ever desired something so bad in life that you willingly overlooked all the red flags? If so, what red flags did you overlook?

_____
_____
_____
_____
_____
_____
_____
_____
_____
_____
_____
_____
_____
_____

2. Are you currently or have you been in a relationship where your partner is abusive (emotionally, mentally, or physically), is cheating on you, lying to you, or just flat out doesn't respect you? _____

   If so, how does this make you feel? _____

   _____

   _____

   _____

   _____

   _____

   _____

   _____

   _____

   _____

   _____

   _____

   _____

   _____

   _____

The Marriage

3. Is your partner a drug user, an alcoholic, or a "social" drunk who gets violent when drinking? _____.
If so, how are you treated when they are under the influence? _____

_____

_____

_____

_____

_____

_____

_____

Is this person abusive to you? _____

_____

_____

_____

Do you have children with this person? _____
If so, are they also being abused? _____

_____

_____

_____

Chapter Seven

A New Start - So I Thought

"Believe in yourself.
You are braver than you think, more talented than you know,
and capable of more than you imagine."
—Roy T. Bennett

A fresh start for our family. We can do this for our two children, I told myself. We are finally here. Wow, it is so hot in Georgia. Why am I seeing cigarettes and cigarette butts with lipstick in my apartment here in Georgia? He explained that he had a gathering before I arrived, and he didn't have a chance to clean up. *Hmm*, okay, I guess. Stay positive, Gwen. He said he wants his family, so trust him and believe what he has told you.

This man really seemed to want this to work. The apartment was temporary. Our house is in the process of being built, and it's in a very good area. I loved how he was putting forth his best effort. The day finally arrived, and we moved into our house! *Lord, it is starting all over again.* This man was staying out all night again, and when he came home, he went upstairs to sleep. *This is crazy!* It was Christmas morning in 1995. I finally busted him in a lie, and the argument began. I went out to his car to get something, and he became enraged. He pushed me into the door and said, "B****, don't be going in my car!" I picked up a bat to get him away from me, and he left me alone. He was still cursing me out when I went to call the police.

  The next thing I knew, he had hit me in the back of my head with the bat that I had put down at the door. My three-year-old was standing there, and he saw the entire incident. I grabbed him and ran into the master bedroom along with my six-month-old, who was hysterically crying. I called the police. I was expecting company for Christmas dinner, and they arrived to see my husband being escorted in handcuffs to a police car. I had a knot on the back of my head, and to this day, my hair will not grow in that spot.

  My three-year-old, who again witnessed this, told strangers he had never met, "My daddy hit my mommy in the head with a baseball bat." It was so embarrassing. He did this for almost a year. I did everything I could to try to explain to him why he shouldn't say this, but he was only three, and he truly didn't understand. While he doesn't talk about it, I still believe that my child suffers to this day from the abuse he witnessed being inflicted on me.

My husband had childhood friends from New York who lived near us, and I opted to go to their house for the night because I was afraid of my husband coming back. I stayed at the friend's house for a week and a half. I ended up going back to my house because I woke one night to the husband kneeling at the side of my bed, trying to pull my pajamas down in an attempt to have sex with me. I stayed at my house for two days, and then I got an apartment for me and my kids because I was terrified of my husband.

During this time, I met my angels here on earth: the Bouies and the Councils. We instantly became family. They loved and took care of my boys like they were their own. I honestly didn't know what it was like being a part of a family that expressed genuine love for everyone they met, but I found it in them. I smile as I am writing this because I remember we would find reasons to get together and cook, play spades, Taboo, Guesstures, sing, and attend church. Estelle got me going back to church. She continuously invited me, and I finally agreed to go. It was as if she knew what I needed at the time, and I am so thankful to her for that.

A New Start - So I Thought

That church journey was almost cut short when I was coming out of the door for the first time and saw my husband's car. The next thing I knew, he was standing right next to me on my left. As I froze in place and stared straight ahead in fear, I recall thinking, *I am never coming back to this church*. The Bouies asked me, "Who was that?" as he went inside for the second service. I remember saying with emphasis, "That was my husband, and I am never coming back here."

Estelle, I miss you and love you dearly. Rest in heaven, Sis!

This man went to everyone I knew in Georgia, asking them to talk to me. He told them how sorry he was and that he loved me and wanted his family back. Once again, being stupid and vulnerable, I took him back, and guess what? I ended up expecting my third child.

Chapter Seven – A New Start—So I Thought
Thoughtful Reflection

1. Are you ignoring the red flags or enduring abuse and disrespect because you're still dreaming about the family or love you want? _____

   _____

   _____

   _____

   _____

   _____

   _____

   _____

   _____

   _____

   _____

   _____

   _____

   _____

2. Have you found yourself hiding their abuse and cheating from your family and friends because you are embarrassed?

_____

Do you tell yourself, "He's going to change?" _____

_____
_____
_____
_____
_____
_____
_____
_____
_____
_____
_____
_____
_____
_____
_____
_____
_____

3. Are your children witnessing (or have your children witnessed) the abuse he is (or has) inflicting on you? ___ If so, is your safety and the safety of your children worth leaving your abuser? _____. Can you explain why?

_____

_____

_____

_____

_____

_____

_____

_____

_____

_____

_____

_____

_____

_____

_____

_____

_____

_____

_____

Chapter Eight

Life After Divorce

"The greatest discovery of all time is that a person can change his future by merely changing his attitude."

—Oprah Winfrey

D*ivorce. Divorce. Oh, heck no!*
These words were not part of my vocabulary, nor did I imagine they would ever be. *Who would have thought that after eleven years, I would throw in the towel?* Listen, I was at the lowest point in my life. I hated my life, I hated my husband, and worse than that, I hated myself for allowing my husband to treat me the way he had over the years. I began to wish I were dead. I was one step away from being locked up in someone's insane asylum.

My self-esteem was at an all-time low. Of course, he helped keep it there by continuously telling me that no one would want me with three kids. He had absolutely no respect for me. I dealt with his coming home whenever he felt he wanted to, women calling him all hours of the night, him being arrested for DUI and solicitation, listening to him tell other women he loved them, and the physical and mental abuse. The straw that broke the camel's back was the child he had with another woman. I was done! I mentally and emotionally checked out of the marriage.

Yes, you heard me correctly—he has another son born in between my two youngest. I was six months pregnant with my youngest child when I got this news. Of course, reading this, you will not be surprised when I tell you that *he* didn't tell me about this. One of his friends told me that, apparently, the girl had begun calling *his* home, trying to find my husband and threatening to take him to court for child support. He denied it right up until the paternity test proved otherwise.

During this time, I was attending church again regularly. I was saved, sanctified, filled with the Holy Ghost, speaking in tongues, and lying awake at night trying to figure out how I could kill this man and get out of this hellhole called life. I was miserable and just wanted to die. At this point in my life, I endured everything for my kids' sake. Mentally, I had left the marriage six years earlier.

I didn't want my kids to grow up like I did—without a father. You see, a part of me was still hoping for that dream, that fairytale of a family. You know that fairytale where you find *that person* (even if he has faults), who loves you for *you*. You start to believe that if he just asks you to marry him, you can change him, and you will live happily ever after. Then, delusions of grandeur inevitably set in, and you believe that your stuff is gold, and it is the "cure-all" answer. He will change, and everything will be alright.

WOMEN OF GOD, DO NOT KID YOURSELVES! The man you bring to the altar is the man you will ultimately take home. God has made us free moral agents with a right to make choices. If a person has not made up in his mind that he wants to change, there is not a thing you can do to change him. *Women, take it from me, trust God and allow Him to bring the right man into your life. It will save you years of anguish and heartache.*

I endured my marriage for eleven years, and one day I came home from church, opened the garage, and got the surprise of a lifetime. My kids froze in their tracks and said, "Mommy, all of Daddy's stuff is gone." If you could have seen their little faces, ridden with sadness, it would have reduced you to tears. *I have to be strong for them* is all that kept going through my mind. We went inside the house, and it looked as if a tornado had gone through it. The house was in shambles.

The kids, being kids, began asking one question after another, most of which I did not have the answers to. All I kept saying to them was, "No matter what has happened, I love you, and your dad loves you too." In the back of my mind, I was saying to myself, *This no-good bastard has left us, and he wasn't even man enough to face us and say he was leaving. What a coward!*

I began cleaning up and trying to put my home back in order. I fed the kids, gave them a bath, and put them to bed for the night. My goodnight hugs and kisses somehow seemed even more meaningful for some reason that night. I guess that was because I was facing an uncertain future, and I wanted my kids to know that everything was going to be alright. When I finally sat down, I realized what time it was. *Whoa*, I thought. *It is 10:00 p.m. The house is finally quiet, and reality has truly set in. This man has left me with three kids.*

I called Estelle Bouie (God bless her soul) because I needed someone to talk to, and it finally happened. All evening, I had been strong for the kid's sake, and now I couldn't control it any longer. I broke down. I cried a river. Life, as I knew it, had come to a screeching halt. Despite everything that he had taken me through in the marriage, this hurt immensely. I shared with Estelle what had transpired and told her I felt I was an emotional wreck. Here I was with three small kids, a thirteen-hundred-dollar mortgage which was obtained based on both of our incomes, a car note, and everyone knows all the other bills and obligations that come with raising kids and maintaining a home. The fear of the unknown was crippling me.

Estelle, being who she was (although quite annoyed with what had happened), encouraged me. As I think now about the words she spoke to me at that moment, tears have formed in my eyes. Estelle said, *"Sis, we are family. I love you, and we will get through this together. We are here for you and the boys."* The hours that night seemed like an eternity, as I was unable to sleep. I got the kids up the next morning, greeting them with my usual hugs and kisses. There was strength in knowing that despite my emotional state, I would not allow them to see me at my weakest point. I was determined to hold it together for them, and I decided I would only speak positive things concerning their dad when they were present, regardless of how I felt.

When my husband left initially, he was giving me a few dollars here and there to help with childcare and some of the other expenses I had. He still had control over me and my household, although he was living with his mistress and not me. About four to five months after he left, he decided he wasn't going to give me any more money, so the burden of caring for our kids had fallen solely on me. I remember saying to him, "If you don't want to take care of your responsibility on your own, then we will let the courts determine how much your obligation will be."

This was my turning point. I began to take back the control of my life that he had held for so long. I filed for divorce. We had to go through mediation, but he refused to negotiate because he did not feel I was entitled to his military retirement. The process of getting this divorce became very long and drawn out. Ultimately, the court ordered him to pay child support until a final divorce decree could be reached. It took almost a year, but the day finally came when we were to appear before the judge to end our marriage. My attorney subpoenaed Estelle and her husband, along with his friend who told me about the other woman and the baby, along with his wife. When my husband looked up and saw who I had brought to court, he called his attorney out of the courtroom and told him to give me whatever it was I was asking for.

Taking the witness stand and being sworn in that morning was quite a nerve-wracking experience. As I raised my right hand and said, "I do," excitement bubbled up inside of me. The judge asked me a few questions, and then he said, "The petition for divorce has been granted." I remember coming down from the witness stand with a huge smile on my face. As sure as God had put breath in my body, I felt as if a burden had been lifted from me. It felt simply awesome! "I am free! I am free!" is all I kept thinking and saying.

This feeling of elation went on for months, and then one day, it hit me. *Hey, I am by myself. I am raising these kids by myself. These bills are crazy, and trying to cover this mortgage is absurd. I can't do this. I don't have anyone to hold me or make love to me. I have needs that are not and cannot be met—this ain't gonna work. I am lonely.*

One would think, after living through eleven years of hell, no one would desire to be back in that relationship, but I did. I needed the assurance of knowing I had someone. In reality, I now know he was my crutch, my security. In other words, he was a comfort zone for me. I knew what to expect from the relationship, so I dealt with everything he dished out. I was treading on new ground, and it scared me. This unfamiliar territory was swallowing me up, and I was losing it.

I continued putting up a front daily and going to church regularly, like I had it all together, and everything was "peachy keen" for me. What my sisters and brothers in the Lord didn't know was that I was really one step away from being committed to a mental institution. I had begun to slip into a state of depression, and I did not want to face that fact. With each day, it became harder and harder for me to get out of bed. All I wanted to do was sleep and cry. I wanted to die.

The only thing that kept me from ending my life was knowing I had to be here for my boys.

My sons' schools called daily because of their behavior. Things got so bad that I recognized the number from each school. When the phone rang and I saw the number, tears began to flow because I already knew the reason for the call. The anger because of our divorce was manifested in their poor behavior at school, although I had them in counseling. It didn't seem to help them. Perhaps what I was going through mentally then contributed—I don't know. God knows I got tired of the counselor telling me, "They are mad at their father, but they are taking it out on you because you are the closest to them." *Excuse me? Sir, fix them because I am going through hell right now!*

I managed to go to work each day, and I know it was the grace of God that kept me from losing my job. I could not function at work. Thank God for my Workflow VW, who had my back and covered me frequently. *VW, you truly don't know how much of a blessing you were to me at that time.* I couldn't remember things, and half the time, I sat at my desk crying over anything that brought additional stress on me. Driving motivators were the kids, their behavior, the constant calls from their schools, finances, and just the empty feeling of being alone. I finally went to my doctor and told her about my situation. She took me out of work because of stress. She gave me some antidepressant medication, which I started taking, but then I stopped. I did not believe I needed any drugs because in my mind, I was not depressed. I refused to accept the fact that it was depression.

My church attendance diminished, as I did not want to be bothered with "church folks." In actuality, I had begun to blame God for letting this happen to me. People from my church would call my home or job, and I would see their name come up on the caller ID. I would not answer. They would leave messages about how they missed me, how they hoped everything was alright, and they asked me to please call when I got the chance. I couldn't talk to them. I couldn't let them see that I didn't have it together.

People, this is a real emotion. Pride will keep us bound up in our own sorrows and unable to receive deliverance. Instead, we have a pity party while we're still bound. This is where the devil wants us. He knows if he can keep us here; he has already won the battle. The devil is a liar! God said He would fight *all* our battles, and in the end, we win!

This sad state of being went on for months with me. One Friday, I was driving to work (doing my usual crying), and the song "I Am God" by Donald Lawrence came on the radio. I began singing and then crying even harder. I arrived at the parking lot at work, dried my eyes, and went inside to proceed through another meaningless day.

When the day was finally over, I came home, fed the kids, and got into bed. I put my headset on and began listening to "I Am God" again. I cried, and then, as clearly as if someone was speaking to me, these words rose up within my spirit:

"See, that is the problem. You know who I am; I am God, but you are refusing to allow Me to be the Lord of your life."

That was a pivotal point for me.

I had not been to church in months, but the following Sunday, I gathered up the strength to attend the service. Praise and worship seemed to be exceptionally high that morning, and it was refreshing to my soul. I needed that. Service began, and the praise team was asked to sing a special song, *My Life Is In Your Hands* by Kirk Franklin. The words of the song radiated in my spirit. At that moment, I believed that I didn't have to worry and didn't have to be afraid. I believed that joy would indeed come in the morning. Finally, I felt that my troubles wouldn't last always.

I stood up with my hands lifted to God, crying uncontrollably. "I love You, Lord; I love You," is all I could utter. When the praise team finished singing, Pastor had an altar call, and he said, "God says, there are some of you who are hurting, and you feel like giving up. God says to cast your cares on Him. Bring it to the altar and leave it."

I went to the altar as if my life depended on it (and it did), and I gave it to God. I began attending church regularly again.

Life as a single mom was rough. I had three "stair-step" kids who did not understand this new situation they found themselves in. I was in survival mode, where I was doing whatever it took to make sure my kids did not feel the brokenness I felt as a child. I was working a full-time job and making around fifty-five thousand dollars a year. To say times were rough would be an understatement. My ends were not meeting. I had a mortgage I truly couldn't afford, a car note, credit card bills, utility bills, and Lord have mercy, three boys who were eating me out of house and home. Until you are in the valley and you're trying to figure out how you are going to pay the bills and feed your kids, you don't know what calling on God is all about. I remember days going to the grocery store, picking up seventy-nine-cent hot dogs, ten-cent ramen noodles, cans of tuna fish, and a loaf of bread just so my kids could have something to eat. By the grace of God, there was always something for them to eat. It may not have been what they wanted, but there was always food on the table, a roof over their heads, and clothes on their backs. Boy, I remember when I would take my last ten dollars and treat them to meals from the Wendy's Dollar Menu. I thought I was doing well when I could do this, and I thought they were satisfied—so much for thinking. *I'll come back to this.*

My kids were growing, and they wanted to be a part of the activities and sports that were taking place at their schools and in the community. It seemed like everything required putting out money to participate. What happened to the days when I was growing up, when you could play sports, and it didn't cost you four and five hundred dollars? (Oh, did I mention that it was per child?) Because I knew the vital role that playing sports had in my life as I grew up (my way of escaping), I was determined to do whatever it took to let my children take part in these activities. There were many days I went without. I also took a second job in order to ensure that I had enough money to pay the fees needed for them to participate. I kept them involved in school, church, sports, and AAU basketball. When I saw my two youngest children struggling in public school, I put them in private schools so they would have smaller class settings, minimizing some of the challenges they were facing in public schools. I know you may be saying, "But you're already struggling financially." I didn't care. I was not going to let my kids down the way I was let down as a child. God gave them to me, and it was my responsibility to take care of them, whatever the cost.

Now, back to that Wendy's story. I was reminiscing with my middle son when he was twenty-three or twenty-four. He told me that he used to still be hungry after he ate the Wendy's meal. This hurt me to my heart because I hadn't known.

I asked him, "Why didn't you tell me?"

He said, "I didn't say anything because I knew you had taken your last money to treat us."

I felt so bad. I began apologizing to him.

He said, "Mom, stop. You did the best you could for us. I have my good work ethic because of you. I saw everything you went through and how hard you worked to make sure we had all we needed. I saw you go without, so we could play school sports and AAU basketball. You don't owe me an apology. I thank you for being there."

I would be lying if I said I don't think about this now and then, but I know it's true—I did the best I could, and I thank God for giving me the strength to make it through that time in our lives. I know beyond a shadow of doubt that if it had not been for the Lord who was on my side, I would not have made it through those trying times.

I know I am not perfect and may have missed the mark many times when raising my boys. Being a single mom, I did my best to instill in them a love for God, a good work ethic, respect for women, chivalry (which is not dead), respect for their elders, respect for themselves and others, as well as a desire to *be* more and *have* more than their parents. Seeing my boys now, I believe I did alright.

Many of you may wonder what happened to the child my ex-husband had outside of our marriage (between my two youngest boys). Well, one summer my ex-husband wanted the kids to come to Virginia, where he lived. I escorted the kids to the gate so they could catch their plane. Lo and behold, my son says, "There goes J (the child)." The kids boarded the plane, and the next thing I knew, J's mother had come over to where I was sitting.

My thought was, *if she says anything crazy, we are going to come to blows right here at this gate.* I wasn't expecting what followed next. The first words out of her mouth were, "I've been wanting to meet you for a long time so I could apologize to you." Then she continued. "I had no idea he was married; he never told me that. He said the house he was building in Fayetteville, Georgia, was for me and him. I now know it was for you and your family. Again, I apologize, and I really want my son to know his siblings."

At this point, my anger toward that innocent child subsided. I vowed to her right then that I would see to it, and it would happen.

Today, J is an integral part of my kids' lives. When we have holiday events and go on family trips, he is always invited. I treat him like he is one of my boys. Most likely, many of you are probably saying, "It couldn't be me!" Well, you are right. I am not you, and what I learned a long time ago is that the child did not ask to be here. He had nothing to do with the actions of my ex-husband and his mother. No, I will not leave any child to be broken because of someone else's actions. He is my kids' sibling, and that makes him a part of my family. He will always be welcome in my house and all events I have for my children.

Chapter Eight – Life After Divorce
Thoughtful Reflection

1. Have you ever had a spouse or a significant other walk out on you and your children? _____

   If so, how did you feel? _____

   _____
   _____
   _____
   _____
   _____

   How did it affect your children? _____

   _____
   _____
   _____
   _____
   _____
   _____
   _____

2. Have you experienced times when you just wanted to be alone, secluded from people who wanted the best from you, experiencing bouts of crying, or just wanting to sleep? _____

   If so, these may be signs of depression. Do you feel as if you may have experienced depression? _____

   _____

   _____

   _____

   _____

   _____

   Have you ever sought opportunities to talk with a therapist or a counselor? _____

   If yes, did it help you? _____

   _____

   _____

   How did it help you? _____

   _____

   _____

   _____

   _____

3. Are you a single mom? _____

   If yes, how are you dealing with your children and their response to the absence of the other parent? _____

   _____

   _____

   _____

   _____

   _____

   _____

   _____

   Are they "acting out," or do you see a change in their behavior since the divorce or separation? _____

   _____

   _____

   _____

   _____

   _____

   _____

   _____

4. If you are struggling to make ends meet, have you reached out to local churches, food pantries, or government agencies? _____

_____

_____

_____

_____

_____

_____

_____

If this applies to you, there are places you can go for help. I encourage you to reach out to someone. There are people and organizations there to assist you. Don't be ashamed of what you're going through. It's the shame that will keep you in bondage and not allow you to seek the help you need to break free.

I know what it's like to have to ask for help. It doesn't feel good. But you deserve better, and your children deserve better. Believe that. Remember, this is just a temporary situation. God will bring you through this.

Chapter Nine

Where the Past Ends, The Future Begins

"The past is behind, learn from it.
The future is ahead, prepare for it.
The present is here, live it."

—Thomas S. Monson

It was a Saturday morning in 2006. I was awakened out of a sound sleep, feeling really sad.

Lord, why am I dreaming about this person? This is now my third dream. I know I hurt him badly when I broke up with him back in 1985. All I desire right now is an opportunity to say I am sorry and give him an explanation about why I broke up with him, which is something I didn't do back then. I owe him this much.

That evening, I picked up the phone and called my mother.

"Mom, are you able to get in contact with his aunt or cousin and get a number for him? I know he is married, but I just want to tell him I am sorry."

My mom hung up, and about ten minutes later, she called me back with a number. *Guys, can you believe I was now scared to call him?*

I told her, "I can't call him. He is married, and I don't want to be disrespectful. I can't do it!"

My mom said, "It's not like you're trying to get back with him. You just want to apologize."

I said, "I know, but I can't do it."

My mom said, "If you won't, I will." She called him and gave him my number.

He called me about twenty minutes later. He said, "I just got off the phone with Ms. Clara (my mom), and you don't have to be afraid to call me. I am no longer married."

We talked into the early hours of the morning. It was like we picked up where we left off in 1985. I apologized and asked for his forgiveness.

For the next six months or so, we tried to rekindle what I had destroyed, but it was never the same. We are still friends to this day, and I will always cherish the friendship and the love we once had.

Seven years later, a mutual friend introduced me to the man who would become my Boaz. Don't get me wrong, it took some time for me to learn this, as I initially tried to cut him off. I remember when he asked me out for the first time. I agreed to go, but I told him I had to go grocery shopping first, so my kids would have something to eat. He said that was fine and he would go with me to the store. I was doing my normal shopping and picking up my seventy-nine-cent hot dogs, ninety-nine-cent bologna, cheap ramen noodles, etc.

He looked at me and said, "What are you doing?"

"Getting food for my kids."

He then asked, "Why are you getting *this* stuff?"

I said, "Look, I'm getting what I can afford."

He looked at me and said, "I want you to put this stuff back. Then I want you to shop like you have the funds to shop. Get what you *really* want your kids to have."

After I did what he instructed me to do, he paid for my groceries. I should have known I had a keeper at that point, but I didn't. I was so damaged at this time; it was hard for me to let my walls down and allow anyone into my life. I didn't trust any man or their motives for wanting to be with me. If a person slightly reminded me of my ex-husband, I called it quits! I recall the night when all of this changed. He had done or said something which I can't recall now, and I tried to end it.

He said, and I quote, "Hold up. Stop. I am *not* your ex-husband. You are a queen, and you deserve to be treated as such."

Urrgghhhh! Say what?

That got all of my attention, and let's just say we are still going strong—sixteen years later. It's not always easy, but learning how to accept each other as we are, respect each other, and communicate with each other has been key.

My husband treats me like his queen, and he goes out of his way to make sure I am taken care of. I am thankful for him and thankful that he constantly shows my boys what a real man is and how they should treat a woman.

I love you, Baby!

Chapter Nine – Where the Past Ends, Future Begins
Thoughtful Reflection

1. Have you ever held on to things of the past that have limited your ability to be present in your "now?" _____ If so, what was your experience? _____

   _____
   _____
   _____
   _____
   _____
   _____
   _____
   _____
   _____
   _____
   _____
   _____
   _____

2. Have negative or hurtful past experiences kept you from embracing or accepting "good" people into your life? ___
If so, how did it affect you? _____

_____

_____

_____

_____

_____

_____

_____

How did it affect them? _____

_____

_____

_____

_____

_____

_____

_____

3. Was there anyone in particular you "pushed away?" _____

   If so, who? _____

Chapter Ten

God Will Never Leave Nor Forsake You

> "Change will not come if we wait for some other person
> or some other time. We are the ones we've been waiting for.
> We are the change that we seek."
> —Barack Obama

I have shared my life story not to call people out but to lift women up. I was broken. I've been abandoned by my father, molested and raped by a caregiver, emotionally separated from a mother who didn't know how to show love, and victimized by multiple domestic violence incidents. The very people who should have been there to protect me were the ones who let me down. The incidents I experienced at a young age caused me to act out in ways that were very unbecoming of a young lady. Being promiscuous, a hardcore drinker, and a person with very low self-esteem who was always trying to validate herself through a man is not who I was meant to be. It is a lifestyle I would not wish on anyone. But through it all, God never forgot about me. I was *Broken But Not Forgotten!*

Perhaps some of you are asking, "Is this story real? Did she really go through all this? Why is she telling it now?"

The truth is—this book isn't for me. I am not here to entertain you or amuse you. I am not perfect, nor do I profess to be. These are the cards I was dealt. This is the life I've had to endure. If anything I've been through or anything I can say will help another person get out of a bad relationship, raise their self-esteem, or more importantly, begin to know God for themselves, then it has all been worth it.

Don't get me wrong, there are times when I might be watching a movie or listening to someone talk about being molested, raped, or abused, and it triggers me. Yes, I will get sad and mad, and I may even shed some tears, but what I tell myself and what I am telling you is that God loves me, and He loves you, too. He is not a respecter of persons. If you look to Him and you are willing to leave your hurt and your brokenness with Him, He will see you through your situation.

That day at the altar, when I left that burden there, I left my past. God had to teach me how to love again. I am not talking about a superficial love. I am talking about "agape," the "God" kind of love.

Merriam-Webster.com defines love as: (1) A strong affection for another arising out of kinship or personal ties, (2) Attraction based on sexual desire: affection and tenderness felt by lovers, (3) Affection based on admiration, benevolence, or common interests."

The Bible tells us that we should have agape love, which is the "God" kind of love. It's unconditional. When you truly learn how to walk in the love God has given us, it doesn't matter what you've been through; you can forgive people. For so long, we have allowed society, friends, family, and predators to dictate who we are or who we should be. It's time for us to take back the control we have given to these people. We can't control what happens to us, but we *can* control how we react to what has been done to us.

In order for us to love someone, we must first love ourselves. God didn't put women on earth to be used or abused by a man, or anyone else, for that matter. He made women to be "helpmeets."

Women, we've got to begin to see ourselves the way God sees us.

I know God looks down on His creation daily, and what He sees saddens Him. Many of our young women have lost their self-respect, and the older generations are allowing it to be. Young women (and heck, older women too) walk around daily half-dressed, gyrating, twerking, giving themselves to anyone who will look, all in the name of being what society feels they should be. We are glorifying immoral and illicit acts and are failing to help and identify people who are hurting and being victimized.

Parents, for the love of God, stop telling your children "what goes on in our house stays in our house!" No! If they are being raped, molested, or abused, it's time to call "time out" on the devil! Give your child a voice and a safe place to land. That means your child knows they can come to you with whatever problem they have, knowing that you have their back and will always be there for them. As a society, we've got to do better.

The question I want you to ponder right now is, "Will you be a victim or a victor?"

A definition of the word *victim* found on Merriam-Webster.com is "one that is subjected to oppression, hardship, or mistreatment." It's often easier to take the route of turning to drugs, alcohol, a life of prostitution or promiscuity, only to numb the pain that dwells within. Constantly seeking that next high and someone to love and accept you are all part of that victim mentality. I get it. I totally understand where you are. Yes, I've been there and can wear the T-shirt to support it. I encourage you to take another stance. Merriam-Webster.com defines the meaning of *victor* as "one that defeats an enemy or opponent: winner."

God knew you before you were formed in your mother's womb. He made you in His image. You have a purpose, and it's time for you to put the devil (that abuser, the molester, the cheater, etc.) under your feet. Call out the evil for what it is, and don't allow the devil to hide! Pick yourself up by the bootstraps and refuse to allow him to have *any* place in your life. The devil is a liar, and *you* are the victor! God gave us free will, which means we have the right to make a choice. Choose today whether you will be a victim or a victor!

You are the sum total of every word that has proceeded out of your mouth. Speak life over your situation. Begin to call on God and see yourself as the individual He has predestined you to be. You are more than a conqueror. You can do all things through Christ, and you are a child of The King! Lay prostrate before the Lord and cast all your cares on Him. He can and He will deliver you from every situation you will find yourself in. I know if it were not for the Lord having been on my side, I would not be where I am today. I love the

Lord with my entire being, and I thank Him for keeping me through everything I've been through.

People see me at church, and I know they're thinking, *Why is she always up praising God and crying? She can't even make it through a song without crying.* Say what you want, I don't care. I know where God has brought me from, and there ain't no devil in hell that will keep me from giving MY GOD all the praise He is due. When you can't form two words to begin a sentence, lift your hands and surrender it all to the Lord. He knows your heart, and He will meet you where you are.

Lord, I pray that You bless the person who is reading this book. I ask that You give them the courage and the strength to lift up their head and open their mouth to give You praise. Bless them to know they may be broken, but they are not forgotten. Allow them to see Your footsteps in the sand, Lord, and know that You are walking every step with them. In Jesus' Name, Amen.

Chapter Ten – God Will Never Leave Nor Forsake You
Thoughtful Reflection

1. Are you sick and tired of feeling "sick and tired?" _____

2. Are you going to continue to be a victim, or will you take your place in society as a victor? What steps will you take to start living life as a victor?

_____

_____

_____

_____

_____

_____

_____

_____

_____

_____

_____

_____

_____

3. You are the total of every word you've ever spoken. Are you ready to change how you speak about yourself and your situation? _____

   What changes will you make to help establish a healthy habit of positive "self-talk?" _____

   _____

   _____

   _____

   _____

   _____

   _____

   _____

   _____

   _____

   _____

   _____

   _____

   _____

Resources

After answering the *Thoughtful Reflection* questions, if you feel you might benefit from the help of professionals who care, please consider using the resources below. Help is available, and you are worth it. These websites and toll-free numbers will lead you to information and help for you, your children, or your loved ones. God bless you!

Alcoholism

    Alcoholics Anonymous

    Website: https://www.AA.org

Counseling and Mental Health Services

    United Way National 211 Directory (2-1-1 Helpline) - 24 Hours

    Call: 211 or 1-800-346-2211

    Mental Health (Adults, Teens, and Children)

    Crisis and Emergencies

    Website: https://www.211.org or 211@uww.unitedway.org

Domestic Violence

National Domestic Violence Hotline – 24 Hours
Call: 1-800-799-7233
Website: https://www.thehotline.org

Parenting

National Parents Organization
Call: 617-431-8019
Website: https://www.sharedparenting.org/mission

Sexual Abuse

RAINN - National Sexual Assault Hotline - 24 Hours
Call: 800-656-4673 or 800-843-5678
Website: https://rainn.org
Online chat: online.rainn.org

Substance Abuse

National Drug Abuse Hotline - 24 Hours
Call: 844-289-0879
Website: https://drughelpline.org

Substance Abuse and Mental Health Services Administration (SAMHSA) — 24 Hours
Call: 800-662-4357
Website: https://www.samhsa.gov

Conclusion

Here's The Deal

> "The key to forgiving others is to
> stop focusing on what they did to you
> and start focusing on what God did for you."
> —Max Lucado

Many of you may be saying, "Wow, she has aired all of her business." That's alright. I am convinced it is time for us to expose the devil as the liar he is. We must let him know he will not continue to have us bound. We, as a people, have grown accustomed to covering up the abuse we have suffered in our lives. It is unfortunate that our inability to communicate these difficult situations is what has allowed the abusers to remain in control and the victims to remain victims. Yeah, you may have been a victim, but you do not have to stay in a victim's state of mind. You are a child of the MOST HIGH GOD, and in Him you can do anything you put your mind to.

I know where you are. I know every emotion you have and may still experience. The abuse (physical and mental) you have experienced is real. The hurt and pain are real. God is a good God, and He has made you more than a conqueror. The

Greater One dwells on the inside of you. You are blessed and highly favored. It is time to change your mind. If you can change your mind, you will inevitably change your life.

Stop blaming yourself and others for the position you find yourself in today. Seek God and His will for your life and follow Him. You can choose to remain where you are and never fulfill the destiny that God has for you, or you can pick yourself up, forgive yourself for the poor choices you've made in the past, and declare, "I am who God says I am! I will not allow anybody to treat me like a doormat, and I am not anyone's punching bag!" If a man cannot love, honor, and respect you for the *queen* you are, then he does not deserve to have you.

Women of God, let him go! Let God bring that man into your life who will complement you, the one who will treat you the way God intended for you to be treated.

Women, we must learn to love, respect, and honor ourselves prior to looking for a fulfilling relationship with a man.

Cherishing ourselves and our bodies, as well as knowing we have been made in God's image, is what our lives should be about. God has made no junk. God knew you before you were formed in your mother's womb. He has ordained your steps, and He knows the plans He has for your life. A great deal of our inability to love ourselves and our insecurities comes from our childhood.

Well, let me speak for myself. If I could talk *to* my younger self, I would say,

"Gwen, as a child, you were not equipped to deal with the trauma you endured, and this manifested itself in your bad attitude and behavior. Forgive yourself and apologize to anyone who has ever been on the tail end of one of your emotional outbursts.

Gwen, it is not your fault that a man contributed sperm to your creation and chose not to have anything to do with you. Whether it was your mother's doing or his, it's not your burden to carry.

To the five-to-nine-year-old Gwen, I want you to know it's not your fault. You didn't ask to be put in a situation that allowed a sixteen-year-old boy to violate you.

More importantly, Gwen, in all your searching for the love you didn't have growing up, you found yourself in an extremely volatile marriage. Please know that the pain he inflicted on you was the demons he failed to deal with from his own childhood. While it is not an excuse for him, it is not your fault, nor is it your burden to carry.

Finally, Gwen, I want you to forgive all the adults who failed you. You know, the people who found it more liberating to talk about how bad your attitude was or how bad you were. Hey, just remember, they talked about Jesus, too. He never did a single thing that was wrong. Who are you to be offended? If those people only knew the hell you endured growing up, or if they had taken the time to try to understand what you were going through, maybe your childhood would have been different. We'll never know. Please believe that true healing comes from God. Continue to seek God and allow Him to deal with the days you find yourself down. You have a big heart and a genuine love for people. Don't let the adverse actions of a few keep you from being the person God has called you to be. I love you."

I know God has ordained this book for such a time as this, and it was He who revealed to me that there are women out there who needed to hear my testimony.

Endorsements

"*Broken But Not Forgotten* is a heartfelt page-turner of surviving continuous unspeakable situations with grace and perseverance through faith. The author tells her story raw and uncut, to speak to readers authentically, relating to them through various chapters of life."—**McKenna Yaple**

* * *

"I found the book to be very (female) empowering, which is awesome! There are a lot of women out there who have gone through similar aspects of your story, and I believe your testimony can shed light on such a major trauma and give females the courage to take back their lives. As vivid as the story might have been, you really welcomed the reader into your life. You showed if one places their trust in God, He will handle all their problems. Life might seem rough as one goes through trials and tribulation, but it isn't the end, and God has a higher purpose for them. You revealed this based on how you depicted your life and the sacrifices you felt you needed to make to provide for and give your kids a better life. For that, Mom, I will forever be grateful and cherish you. I work hard to hopefully one day give it back to you and instill it into my kids. You still continue to show up for us, even today. You did a great job, Mom, you should be proud!" —***Donte Lay***

* * *

"This book made me feel more connected to the author and my own experiences I have endured in the past. Even though I have forgiven those who hurt me, it let me know how much I really have and who I am today because of it. When my mom was alive, we had a good relationship. To read about the author's mother having men coming in and out and not having the capacity emotionally to relate to her lets me appreciate my mom even more. This book is a good read. It opens your eyes to where you are today, whether it is healing you need or being thankful you have overcome your own adversities. THIS BOOK IS A MUST READ!" —***Wendy Ward***

* * *

"A deeply moving story, one that delves into the heart of resilience and strength in the face of adversity. This book highlights not just the hardships of a young girl's life but also the incredible inner power and growth that can emerge from difficult circumstances. Knowing that it is a personal narrative forces the incidents to leave a lasting impact, inspiring empathy and understanding. I am genuinely touched by this book and how it will help others, and also allow my wife to fulfill her divine responsibility. I love you, Dear!" —***Roger A. Bain Sr.***

* * *

"This book is a celebration of women's strength, resilience, and capacity for love even in the darkest of times. It's a must read for anyone who has endured abuse, and I hope it honors the untold stories of women." —***RJ Lay***

* * *

"This is a heartfelt but real story told by a relatable individual. I love how Gwen is able to utilize scripture to not only overcome but also motivate others in their journey as well. This book is an inspiration to all, as there is a message for everyone within." —***Bryant Lay***

About the Author

Gwendolyn N. Bain was born and raised in Westbury, New York. She is married to Roger Bain, and they are a blended family with a total of five children. Gwen is a mother of three, and Roger is a father of two.

Gwen has earned a Bachelor of Science with a major in Marketing Management and a Master of Arts in Business Administration with a major in Human Resources. Her current career is in the field of Business Continuity. This enables her to help companies become resilient by anticipating and preparing for events that could impact people, companies, assets, etc. As Gwen wrote her bio, she realized how ironic it was that *resiliency* is a highlight in her current career. As she reflected on her experiences, it was amazing to recognize the resilience she has carried throughout her entire life.

"Coming to know God and trusting Him throughout the writing process has given me the courage to share my testimony with you. I hope you will find solace in my words, God through my faith, and the help you may need to change your life."

—*Gwendolyn N. Bain*

THANK YOU

Thank you for taking the time to read my book.
Your support means the world to me.

If you find value or insight from
Broken But Not Forgotten:
Finding Strength in Faith Through Life's Deepest Wounds

I would be incredibly grateful if you would send a review to gwen@lyricallybain.com. I will share your feedback and personally respond to your email.

Your feedback helps me improve as I continue my career as an author
and allows other potential readers to discover my book.
Simply send an email and share your thoughts:
gwen@lyricallybain.com

Thank you once again for your support and for joining me on this journey.

God bless you,

Gwendolyn N. Bain